# Not Done Yet

*The Extraordinary Legacy of an Ordinary Woman*

CAROL VANKIRK

ISBN 979-8-89043-067-0 (paperback)
ISBN 979-8-89043-068-7 (digital)

Copyright © 2024 by Carol Vankirk

All rights reserved. No part of this publication may be reproduced, distributed, or transmitted in any form or by any means, including photocopying, recording, or other electronic or mechanical methods without the prior written permission of the publisher. For permission requests, solicit the publisher via the address below.

Christian Faith Publishing
832 Park Avenue
Meadville, PA 16335
www.christianfaithpublishing.com

Printed in the United States of America

# CONTENTS

Introduction .................................................................. v
Prologue ...................................................................... vii

Chapter 1:  My Story
            How My Curiosity Led Me to God ........................ 1
Chapter 2:  I Would Have Despaired
            Understanding How God Works ......................... 9
Chapter 3:  To Feel Rejection
            (An Original Poem) ......................................... 11
Chapter 4:  He Has His Ways
            It's Okay That He's All Powerful and We are Not ..... 12
Chapter 5:  His Magnificent Creation
            Finding So Much More in the Creation
            Story Than Just the Creation ............................ 14
Chapter 6:  The Will of God and the Will of Man
            Two Mindsets at Odds ..................................... 18
Chapter 7:  The Shepherds' Christmas Story
            Their Amazing Decision ................................... 20
Chapter 8:  Our Christmas Challenge
            Keeping Christ in Christmas ............................ 22
Chapter 9:  Christmas Thoughts
            (An Original Poem) ......................................... 24
Chapter 10: The Mystery of His Wounds
            Why Did Jesus Have to Suffer So Much on
            the Cross? ..................................................... 26

Chapter 11: The Book of Habakkuk
God's Simple but Profound Answer to
Habakkuk's Distress ..................................29
Chapter 12: Watch, Stand Fast, Be Brave
A Closer Look at 1 Corinthians 16:13.....................35
Chapter 13: Songs in the Night
God's Goodness in the Middle of a Sleepless Night ......39
Chapter 14: The Anchor for Our Soul
God's Gift of Hope in Troubled Times .....................41
Chapter 15: Our Wonderful Counselor
Our Wounded Souls Can Be Healed ........................43
Chapter 16: A Lamp for My Feet
You Can Know Where You're Going .....................47
Chapter 17: Psalm 139:13–16
God is Passionately Preparing Every Life for Purpose....49
Chapter 18: My Prayer of Thanksgiving
Thoughts on God's Eternal Word and How
It Has Changed Me....................................................50
Chapter 19: Be Anxious for Nothing
A Most Wonderful Blessedness Can Be Ours............53
Chapter 20: The Whole Armor of God
Teaching Us How to Fight the Spiritual
Battles on Earth...................................................55
Chapter 21: The Book of Job
(The Amazing Ending)................................................59
Chapter 22: That Big Beautiful Moon
My Special Song in the Night..................................64
Chapter 23: Consider This
Short Snippets of Thoughtful Things .......................66
Chapter 24: The Story of the Prodigal Son
You Can Always Come Home .................................71

Epilogue........................................................................75

# INTRODUCTION

    The idea of leaving something of myself behind after I am gone started niggling at my heart a long time ago. At first, I didn't pay much attention to it, but over the last several years, it has become something that I've gotten more serious about and want to accomplish in my life. I realize that I have been given a beautiful, invaluable gift, and I want to tell you about it. God has walked with me for over fifty-five years and has taught me things that have given my life purpose and value. I want to tell you how my faith has grown over the years and how much God has blessed me and been faithfully by my side. My story sheds light on the unlimited possibilities afforded to each human being. God promised that what He began in me all those years ago, He is faithful to complete (Philippians 1:6 NKJV), and that's why I chose the title of this little book to be *Not Done Yet*. I am still a work in progress. But there's even more to *Not Done Yet*. The scripture from the Psalms says it so beautifully to all of us: "One generation will declare Your works to the next and will proclaim Your mighty acts" (Psalm 145:4 CSB). We have a job to do.

    So let me begin, and may God be glorified as His faithfulness, grace, and mercy are revealed in these pages.

# PROLOGUE

I'm glad you're here. I hope you will enjoy this little book. It begins by telling my story how God and I met and all the ways He taught me so much about Himself through specific challenging times in my life. The rest of the book is simply my thoughts about various Scripture verses that I have underlined in my Bible over the years. Each verse, each truth can meet the need of any moment in any life. It's amazing. I hope you will enjoy reading about this magnificent God of ours and His loving involvement with those who open their hearts to Him. God bless you.

# CHAPTER 1

# My Story

### How My Curiosity Led Me to God

When I was about twelve years old, I started to wonder where people went when they died. This might be considered a bit odd for a twelve-year-old, but there it was…front and center in my mind. And just like a loving Father, He was going to reveal that and much more to me over the rest of my life. However, it would take several years to really get my attention again.

I didn't grow up hearing about a personal relationship with God nor about spiritual things in general. We went to church when we felt like it and usually left the service feeling glad it was over…at least, that was how I felt.

Years passed, and then one night, I was home alone watching a Billy Graham Crusade on TV. *He told me what I needed to do to become a Christian: repent and accept the free gift of salvation through Jesus's death, burial, and resurrection.* And so I prayed to God for the salvation He was offering, and that night, I became a Christian—a child of God. I didn't realize how profound and life-changing that was going to be. God had begun to reveal Himself to me more and more, and over the years, He has taught me many priceless lessons. He began this journey by teaching me one very valuable lesson. If I was surrendering my life to Him as I became a Christian, that meant to God that I surrendered everything. But I held back one area of my life. I was afraid I wouldn't like it if He asked me to go to China as a missionary, so I never fully said yes to Him. I didn't know why I felt this way and why it scared me so, but it was enough that I just couldn't surrender all to Him.

For years, God patiently waited until finally, one day, I knelt in front of my bed and told God that if He wanted me to be a missionary in China, I would go, but that He would have to explain it to my now husband and children because they would not understand. I had given up the last hold I had on my life, and I can tell you I had such a sense of freedom, and peace came over me. Much to my relief, God didn't ask me to go to China at all. He just wanted to know that I was all His. I began to see glimpses of God's character in all of this:

1. *He understands our fears and weaknesses and is patient and kind.* He doesn't usually fulfill our fears, only His will. If we should be afraid, He is faithful to give us what we need to be obedient despite the fear. It was so encouraging to know that God's patience could help me make the right decision.

One of my earliest struggles was giving time to God by praying and reading the Bible. Good intentions soon gave way to frustration and then to forgetting God or, at the very least, keeping Him waiting. This went on for quite some time. Satan was successful at keeping me away from hearing God's voice, and that was because I didn't recognize Satan's methods. I thought it was only me failing, but in reality, I came to understand that both Satan and the Holy Spirit wanted my attention in order to influence me. Not understanding the spiritual warfare waging around me, I chose, by not choosing, to hear Satan's voice in my ear.

Early on in my married life, God used our early struggles to help me notice the lack of peace I had and the feelings of helplessness and hopelessness. But He was faithful to me and was unwilling to leave me alone there. Someone invited me to a women's Bible study, and I went. It was there that I began to learn so many things about God. I have been in Bible studies ever since. Having a quiet time to read the

Bible and pray was difficult timewise, but I was doing better. Again, I saw something in God's character that I hadn't known before:

2. *He shows us compassion in our times of personal struggle when consistency is difficult. I never felt judged—only loved, and it made all the difference.*

I always yearned to be a prayer, and God saw that in my heart. Encouragement to pray came as an event that lasted two years and broke my heart. Bob was in anesthesia school in Wisconsin, and we lived in an apartment complex that all the other students lived in as well. We were all married and had children. One of the wives took a dislike to me and began a whispering campaign behind my back about me and my children—more specifically about my oldest child. One by one, the other children were told not to play with him. Puzzled, I went to this woman, thinking she was a friend, to talk to her about what was going on. She pretended to be sympathetic and ignorant of the situation. Things got worse, and I was devastated. None of the other wives had much to do with me. None of the children could play with our oldest child. God took this terrible time and did several amazing things.

First, I had told everyone I was a Christian, only because I thought they were too, so now they knew and would watch to see how I handled things. God was going to use this time to bring glory to Himself. But it was difficult, and I often shed tears because I couldn't really see what He was doing at first. I didn't really understand God that well, and it seemed like He didn't care. I only felt the pain of rejection. I went to the scriptures and read and underlined, all the while asking God to speak to me. I really struggled to understand why God didn't just step in and do something that made sense to me. But He had other plans, and I needed to get on board. I slowly began to depend on Him to give me guidance and to just meet what needs I had. But He went beyond that.

Here's what He did. Since my son couldn't play with any of their kids, God soon provided other kids living in the same complex as us who came over to play. He opened up so many opportunities to love them and share this loving God—whom I was getting to know—with them and just to be different from all the other adults in their lives who didn't know God and were living pretty tough lives just surviving. This was one of the first times in my life I experienced God turning evil intensions into something good. I have remembered that all these years and have seen it happen again and again. God is so good.

I stayed kind to all the women and their children as much as I could, and before we left there, they told me they could see that I wasn't awful like had been said about me. But the most amazing thing that happened was when the woman behind all of the troubles had to have surgery, I went to visit her in the hospital. As I was leaving, she apologized to me, and out of my mouth came the words, "That's alright. I've already forgiven you." It was so surreal to say those words, but then, they weren't really mine. It was God's, and it became a huge witness of what God can do when we are hurt if we seek Him rather than take revenge. And again, I learned something about God's character:

3. *Love, forgiveness, and trust are priceless in God's eyes. He taught me just how priceless these three things are when I was most vulnerable, and, looking back, I can see how right His timing was.*

That long trial was over.

Life went on, and troubles came and went. My faith continued to grow through Bible study, prayer, and time with my Christian friends. Always, God was preparing me for the next trial, but He was also showing me how to enjoy life more as well. I always tended to be a worrier, fearful, gloom and doom, and all those "lovely" things. I needed to learn that my life really would be okay no matter what happened, and I needed to enjoy God. I would drift away from consistently praying and reading the Word so often that Satan could easily take my weakness and make me miserable and afraid and depressed. For me, it had been a struggle. Identifying the cause (that is, my personality, my distance from God, and Satan's influence) had helped me seek God much sooner and helped me stop listening to

Satan, loudly speaking these accusations that all was bad and hopeless. Isn't it wonderful that God *always* gives us a way to defeat evil?

One of the things that I really didn't trust God with was my children. I could let Him have His way with me more and more, but I just didn't trust that He would care for my children gently enough. I thought He might do something drastic, and I needed to hold on to them so I could protect them from anything horrible. Looking back, it was all so silly to think that this powerful God would not take good care of my children. I was just a grasshopper thinking I was a lion. Nothing devastating ever happened to our children despite my foolish trepidation.

When my children finally were all in school and Bob worked all day, I developed the habit of doing a Bible study lesson and then praying from a prayer list. These were the best times of consistency, which further prepared me for the next series of trials. Each trial was difficult enough to teach me one more characteristic of God and one more area to go into spiritually. I was involved in the church that we attended and met with legalistic leaders, who really didn't like me. I think they felt threatened that their leadership style was wrong as I challenged it. I was lied about, and eventually, a potential character assassination took place. Instead of running away, I confronted them. They really had hoped I would be so upset that I would quit the church, but I wasn't going to do that until I made it clear that I didn't fear their lies. God was there and judgment occurred.

I eventually left with a good conscience, and in a few more years, the church was forced to close its doors…everyone was gone. But the best thing was that I was able to leave there forgiving them, not hating them. I learned that God holds my reputation, not man. God calls me into account. There is quite a bit of freedom in that. God doesn't destroy us… He changes us. Man tries to destroy and then walks away. Knowing this takes away fear. I suffered through tears and anger before it was all over, but in the end, I learned that if God is for us, who can be against us? My lessons always involved tears and, sometimes, anger or both. But God was so faithful to bring me through to the other side, where I understood a little bit more about Him. I loved that.

Fast forward a bit. Back in 2005, I could have lost my husband, Bob, to a massive heart attack. The doctor told me that without bypass surgery, he was days away from a massive heart attack, and he would not survive. God didn't take him then, but the path we had to walk included being blindsided with this heart issue, consequent bypass surgery, and six weeks without any income as he recovered. My first reaction when I heard the doctor say he couldn't work for six weeks was, "What will we live on?" Bob was self-employed at the time, so there was no paid sick leave. In the next instant after fear, I made a decision to simply trust God with every need. I had forgotten that years, before when Bob was in anesthesia school, we didn't have much money, yet God provided for our daily needs. He never failed us then, and I believed He wouldn't fail us now. He took care of us beyond our needs. It was beautiful to see and receive. My faith was growing, and my understanding of how God cares for us was also growing.

*4. He was teaching me to trust Him and to stay faithful. Soon, He was going to teach me a far better way to see things that would completely change everything for me.*

He allows pain and struggles in our lives for a greater good. Sometimes, we can't understand why at the moment, so I've learned to look for something else in His character to help me get through tough, unexplainable times. I realized that an eternal perspective, His perspective, would be far better than the worldly one I had, so I asked Him to let me see the things that were happening in my life through His eyes. I was amazed how my perspective changed everything. I learned that He sees with compassionate eyes, and I needed to see that way too. Seeing from a heavenly perspective is powerful and profound. We, by default, see things from a worldly perspective, but oh, the joy and healing that can come from seeing as God sees. Satan wants to destroy all of us, but God wants to heal and redeem. I've never forgotten how one's perspective is so powerful. I praise God for His blessed faithfulness. He is a very good and gracious Father, and I love Him.

God is always at work in our lives, and I learned that I don't have to see what He is doing to believe He's doing something. His faithfulness to us all is unending. My faith in believing, even though I can't see it, is pleasing to God. Scripture says that it is impossible to please God without faith (Hebrews 11:6 CSB). That's a pretty profound statement. Impossible is a pretty strong word, but when I thought more about it, I understood why it's true. I think an intricate part of faith is trust, and it is foundational in my relationship with God—in fact, in any relationship. I am still learning about my relationship with God. He is never petty, nor does He do mean things as if He doesn't care. So if things should appear to be so, I tell myself this is one more thing I simply don't understand, and I've learned to look at God rather than the circumstances around me. Circumstances can make God look inept or uncaring or mean to us. He is not any of those things. *Everything* God does is done out of an unending love for us. He leads us through His perfect plan for our lives. He generously gives peace and joy that we cannot explain while bringing glory to Himself as He so clearly deserves. We have an amazing God, who is always good, full of compassion, tender-hearted, and merciful.

I never realized all that God planned to do in my life after I became a Christian. His forgiveness of my sin set me free and changed the course of my life. He has shown me His love and compassion, a path that leads heavenward, and a hope that doesn't disappoint. He has taken away fear of the unknowns in life and taught me that I am to live by faith—faith in an unshakable, unchangeable God, whose love I cannot escape. He is everything.

Over the first few years of being a Christian, God gave me a path to follow, which has helped keep me on the right path and which will ultimately lead me home. It's for all of us.

1. Read the Bible, and discover its truths, and let Him equip you for the spiritual battle.
2. Ask for wisdom and understanding.
3. Be in a Bible study as often as possible.
4. Be with like-minded friends.
5. Attend church regularly.

6. Get to know the character of God—His attributes.
7. Pray, trust, and wait for Him in all things.

He showed me layers of life as I grew more consistent to do these things. My prayers came quicker, my trust grew surer, and in the waiting, I came to see the bigger picture God was always working on. But most of all, I began to see a most beautiful God, who loves us, fights for us, blesses us, comforts, guides, and directs us. I am slowly being made into the person God made me to be. I know I have a blessed and secure future ahead as He is enabling me to be stronger and more victorious every day. He's just that kind of God.

# CHAPTER 2

# I Would Have Despaired

## Understanding How God Works

I would have despaired unless I had believed
that I would see the goodness of the Lord in the
land of the living; wait for the Lord; be strong,
and let your heart take courage; yes, wait for the Lord.

—Psalm 27:13–14 NASB

I was going through one of those times in my life when things were not as I hoped they would be. But that's life, isn't it? I had been praying for resolution and healing, and nothing was happening. I think I was feeling discouraged until I read these verses. The most important word for me in them was "believed." That is so fundamental to my relationship and knowledge of God…that is what propels my faith. I understood the "goodness of the Lord in the land of the living" meant that God was working with me and other Christians in what was going on. His goodness was what brought healing. I knew that waiting for the Lord was imperative for the growth of my faith. It's so fundamental and life-changing to know that He is faithful but will take whatever time is needed to answer our prayers. Belief in His goodness and waiting makes us stronger and less afraid of what might lie ahead. I found that He not only addresses the problem, but

He also gives us personal growth in the process…something to pass on to others, something to lean on for the next time, and something to add to what I already know of His character. God truly offers each one of us all sufficiency for all of life. Praise His name!

# CHAPTER 3

# To Feel Rejection

## (An Original Poem)

To feel rejection
    Is to feel the deepest pain.
To keep on loving
    Is to reach the highest plane.

To know deep sorrow
    Is to know a broken heart.
To keep on trying
    Is to play the hardest part.
To have God's joy
    Is to have an inner calm.
To feel His love,
    Is to feel a healing balm.

No matter what
    This life may give to me
From Him comes strength
    Each day sufficiently.

# CHAPTER 4

# He Has His Ways

## It's Okay That He's All Powerful and We are Not

> "For My thoughts are not your thoughts,
> Nor are your ways My ways," declares the Lord.
> "For as the heavens are higher than the earth,
> So are My ways higher than your ways
> And My thoughts than your thoughts."
>
> —Isaiah 55:8–9 NASB

So what exactly does that mean in the day-to-day prayer life of a believer? And what does it mean that His ways are "higher" than mine? Well, I think it might mean that God has all the answers, all the knowledge, all the insight, all the everything, and I have only a piece of the great puzzle called life. Instead of being disappointed that He doesn't do things the way I think they should be done, I should be ecstatic that it is He, the all-knowing God, who holds everything in His hands and who makes the decisions and not me, the illiterate child. What I have observed, too, is that prayers are answered but often only after many things come together—when the ground work has been laid, when the Holy Spirit has spent time reasoning with the sinner, pointing out their futile chasing after the wind as they continue to be unfulfilled and on and on.

To say we human beings are complex is an understatement, so clearly there's lots of work to do before the answer can finally come. There must be an untwisting of knots, a soothing of emotional pain, an undoing of misguided ideas, and a recognition of emptiness inside. While things are being sorted out, I don't want to be that fussing child in the corner impatiently waiting…no, I want to be that faithful child, thanking Him for what He's doing when I don't even know what that is. I want to be that child of the King, giving honor to Him while I sit without a visible answer yet. I want God to see that I choose to trust Him.

When I'm in His shadow, I have found it to be a beautiful place for abundant spiritual growth, and I love it. It lifts the burden of thinking that it is me and not God who must make things right for others. It is a place where I can sleep the sleep of the child and where I gather strength rather than grow weary. It is a place that I find His grace, and I am forever grateful. I pray big, bold prayers because I know I can, and He is able and willing to answer. He is such an awesome God, and we are blessed that there is *nothing* we can do to cause Him to stop loving us or caring for and about us. But I will still sometimes struggle to understand Him, and when that happens, I think about these words from Charles Spurgeon:

> God is too good to be unkind
> Too wise to be mistaken
> And when we cannot trace His hand
> We must trust His heart.

We truly can trust His heart, and that makes believing in Him a safe thing to do. He will never betray us or fail us. It's a good place for our souls to be.

# CHAPTER 5

# His Magnificent Creation

## Finding So Much More in the Creation Story Than Just the Creation

Genesis 1:1–31 NKJV

*Day One*: In the beginning, God created the heavens and the earth. The earth was without form and void; and darkness was on the face of the deep. And the Spirit of God was hovering over the face of the waters. Then God said, Let there be light and there was light. And God saw the light that it was good; and God divided the light from the darkness. God called the light Day and the darkness He called Night. So the evening and the morning were the first day.

*Day Two*: Then God said, Let there be a firmament in the midst of the waters and let it divide the waters from the waters. Thus God made the firmament and divided the waters which were under the firmament from the waters which were over the firmament… And He called the firmament Heaven…the second day.

*Day Three*: He separated the waters below the expanse, and dry land appeared. He called that earth. This caused the waters to gather with boundaries and He called that seas. Then God made vegetation with its own seed and filled the earth.

*Day Four*: God put the sun and the moon in place to separate the day from the night, for signs and seasons, and for days and years and also to give light on the earth. He made two great lights, the greater light to govern the day, and the lesser light to govern the night. He made stars also. These were placed in the expanse.

*Day Five:* God filled the seas with life and the sky with life. The oceans are filled with fish and other creatures. The skies are filled with birds of all kinds. He told these living creatures to be fruitful and multiply.

Day Six: God said let the earth bring forth living creatures after their kind—cattle and creeping things and beasts of the earth after their kind. *Then God said, let us make man after our likeness and let them rule over the fish of the sea and over the birds of the sky and over the cattle and over all the earth and over every creeping thing that creeps on the earth. So God created man in His own image; in the image of God He created him; male and female He created them... He formed man from the dust of the ground and breathed into his nostrils the breath of life and man became a living being.* God blessed them and told man to be fruitful and multiply and fill the earth and subdue it and rule over the fish of the sea and over the birds of the sky and over every living thing that moves on the earth.

*Day Seven:* This day, God rested. Everything He made was very good, and He was satisfied.

There is so much in this story of the creation. It speaks to the awesome power of God to create life. Nothing was just an inanimate object. Everything, including vegetation, was living and alive.

Everything had its seed for generational new life...its beginning and its end. The details of everything He made, their interconnectedness, the colors, the instincts that caused animals to procreate and care for their offspring, and to find or build shelters is unlike anything else. And it goes on as we have the seasons, the continual growth of all things, the circle of life that doesn't change, the consistency of all things to do what they were created to do—to climb or to dig, to swim or to walk, to fly or to crawl.

But then came His crowning achievement when He created man. He breathed into his nostrils the breath of life and *man became a living being*. He did not breathe life into any other created being—only the one created in His own image. Nothing else that has been created has been created in the image of God. We are different. We have a soul, a mind that has a conscience, a heart that can do good or evil, and a free will to choose our own path or follow God's plan, and the capacity to sin and need a Savior. Plants just exist, animals follow instincts, but man thinks.

God created man and woman. In His creation of woman, He didn't form her out of the dust like He did man. Instead, He chose to include Adam's rib as part of woman's creation. Why did He do it this way? I think the answer is found in these verses: "And the Lord God fashioned into a woman the rib which He had taken from man and brought her to the man. And the man said, 'This is now bone of my bones and flesh of my flesh; She shall be called Woman because she was taken out of Man.' *For this cause,* a man shall leave his father and mother and shall cleave to his wife, and they shall become *one flesh.*" This, I believe, is a picture of the intimacy of a close bond made for mankind within a marriage. Later in the scriptures, God uses marriage between Himself and His church as representing the intimate and close bond God wants with His church, those who have become His children through the blood of Jesus. This remains a beautiful and sacred concept even today, but which sinful man has greatly diminished.

I often think about the things that God created for sheer creativeness and for our pleasure. For example, the butterfly's wings didn't have to be so intricate and beautiful and different from specie to specie in order to function, but how we marvel at them. The tiniest insect has purpose, just like the largest creature with the most intelligence. Everything has meaning and purpose. This has confirmed to me that we also have meaning and purpose for living, no matter what others tell us or what we tell ourselves. There is nothing that God created that He does not love nor is here by accident.

When the sixth day of creation was completed, God looked around and saw that everything was very good and He was satisfied, and then on the seventh day He rested. The meaning of the word *rested* from the original language is not about being tired. It means He simply stopped creating. There wasn't anything else, and there never would be. God never second guessed Himself. He never said,

"Oops, I forgot something." He was completely finished with everything, including mankind. And because God knows everything, God knew man would sin and need a Savior if he was to be with God eternally.

That in itself speaks volumes about God's love for us. He knew man would make a mess of this world and that evil would prevail all too often, and yet He put man in charge of all that He had created. The value and love He has given us is more than our sins could ever be. So the story of creation ended with the seventh day, but the story of redemption was just beginning. Our God is an amazing God whose love for us moved Him to do the unthinkable… He was going to rescue us from spiritual death and separation with the shed blood of Jesus, His only Son.

# CHAPTER 6

# The Will of God and the Will of Man

### Two Mindsets at Odds

God, ever compassionate, has given man a will of his own. I think God wanted us to choose to love Him, so He gave man a means by which to make his own decisions. God's will wants us to be His, to respond to His pursuit of us, and to respond to Jesus's sacrifice for us. He doesn't want to lose us in the end. But He knows He'll lose many of us. He tells us in His Word that the right road is the narrow road, and few will find it. But His love compels Him to take that risk anyway. Man will often tell God, "You don't exist" or "I don't want you running my life" or "I've got things I want to do first," and on and on.

Here's the sad reality: as long as we have life on earth, God's love will compel Him to keep trying to persuade us to choose Him. He blesses all people, and the sun shines on the good and the evil. But when we die, if we still haven't chosen God as our Lord and Savior, then God must walk away and with Him, the essence of who He is leaves too. And who is He? He is love, compassion, joy, peace, forgiveness, patience, Savior, light, hope, gentleness, goodness, healing, King of kings, Mighty Counselor, and Prince of Peace, to name a few things.

And when man chooses to reject God and dies, he will live forever without the essence of God. Now, he will be utterly alone, full of hatred, uncaring, joyless, warring, unforgiven, impatient, in darkness, and hopelessness, evil, will have no love, and will be in sickness, to name a few things. This is hell. God never sends people there. They, by choosing to want a life without God, will find themselves there…a place where God's essence will never be. All that beauty and love will be lost to the one who willfully abandons God. And it's forever.

Thank you, God, that You don't just let us reject you without fighting for us. Oh, that men would not be so foolish as to reject You.

# CHAPTER 7

# The Shepherds' Christmas Story

## Their Amazing Decision

I read once again the Christmas story in the Bible, but this time, I was struck by the part the shepherds played. The cast of characters surrounding the birth of Jesus was in itself quite amazing. A young teenage virgin engaged to Joseph, a carpenter, only a feeding trough to lay Jesus on in a cave for animals. And the first to see Him were shepherds…considered the lowliest of all people. And then when the angels appeared to the shepherds and told them about the birth of Jesus and where He could be found, a truly amazing thing happened that speaks to each of us still today.

The shepherds went in haste to Bethlehem, and in doing so, they left their sheep unprotected. This is the part of the story where I saw something more for the first time. They were in the fields keeping watch over their sheep, but the good news was so amazing that they totally forgot about the sheep's safety and just hurried to Bethlehem.

That's the kind of response God needs from us…don't count the cost, just go! But far too often, I think we humans count the cost first before we respond. But these shepherds believed the angels and went straight to Bethlehem without hesitation. Think what they would have missed had they counted the cost…seeing the King of kings, Lord of lords, and the promised Savior.

# CHAPTER 8

# Our Christmas Challenge

### Keeping Christ in Christmas

Sometimes, I wish we humans never had started gift giving at Christmas. It casts a shadow over God's gift of Jesus as we busy ourselves with shopping, often spending more than we should. I wish it is more like Thanksgiving, where it's about family and friends and time together…gathering around the table for a feast and thinking about the blessings we have received from God. But it is not that way, so our challenge is always to bring Christ back into the conversation, again and again, and to pray for peace, not chaos, during this blessed time of year.

God never intended Christmas to be a hectic time of the year but rather one of peaceful remembrance of the greatest gift anyone could ever receive. To think that such royalty as God Himself humbling Himself and becoming a baby in a stable, where animals live and only lowly, despised shepherds were there to greet him is quite amazing. To think about His testimony to us all of who God is and what truth He speaks that is never changing but always the same for every generation. How comforting that is in a world that changes all too often, where truth is lied about constantly or ignored or applied with no consistency. How wonderful to bring sure footing to any who wants it. And the fact that He never turned back, never quit, and never ceased to care about us as He was betrayed and put on a cruel, humiliating cross for all to see and mock. It's an amazing story and should never have to live in the shadow of any other thing. May God bless this and all Christmases yet to come, with the glory of what He did for us

May that story never be kept in the shadows but always be put on full display for all to see.

# CHAPTER 9

# Christmas Thoughts

(An Original Poem)

Oh, the glory that came down that day,
The humble precious child.
He brought a hope to all the world.
This Savior meek and mild.

Oh, the glory that came down that day
As angels sang such praise,
When the tiny little babe was born
That first of Christmas days.

The Holy Child was here at last,
But known by just a few;
Wrapped only in a pauper's sheet
No kingly garments knew.

Today the story's much the same;
So few will shout for joy.
So many do not want to know
That little baby boy

## NOT DONE YET

He came prepared for what we'd do
He knew what we would say;
That many then and many now
Would turn and walk away.

But some have seen the Glory
That came down that day to rest
The greatest gift there ever was,
The day God gave His best.

And some will sing and shout for joy
And spread the news around.
And so for them on Christmas day
He'll wear His kingly crown.

# CHAPTER 10

# The Mystery of His Wounds

## Why Did Jesus Have to Suffer So Much on the Cross?

Those very words were written in the daily devotional I was reading. What does it mean? The topic was about growing in the grace and knowledge of Jesus. Have you ever wondered why, when Jesus came to die for our sins, He had to die such a cruel and painful death? Why the humiliation? Why the intense suffering, not only physical but spiritual, when God looked away? Why, to save so few when many have/will reject His sacrifice? I'll have to think about this. I'm not sure why He had to suffer so intensely for sinners. Does that speak to His intense, enduring unconditional love? I don't know. What have I missed? How can I ignore the depth of what He did? How can I just say the words without much emotion or gratitude for His suffering? I no longer am destined for hell when my body dies—that place of darkness and aloneness, without sympathy or grace, mercy or love.

Just as much as we often don't grasp the intensity of His sacrifice, I do not grasp the horror of hell and the concept of eternity. This makes me think of the way I see the world we live in. Too often, I see only what's up close "in my world," so to speak. Study of this planet we live in reveals breathtaking enormity and complexity. Its beauty is astonishing. Nature is so in tune with itself. When I look at the night sky or a stormy sky or a beautiful blue sky, I forget this is but a speck in the galaxies, and yet it is complete in itself. It's beautiful and magnificent. It affects our lives in so many ways, on so many levels. There is nothing more that can be added to it or to nature or to our own existence. And to think that sin has devastated humankind, but there is still order in the universe and on the earth. There is still incredible beauty, incredible resources. I cannot destroy what God has made. I could not stop His death on the cross. I cannot save myself. What can I do? I can believe in God almighty, in His Son, Jesus Christ, and listen to the voice of His Holy Spirit. I can draw close to Him and learn from Him, obey Him. I can live as if this place is not my home but rather, heaven is the home I am traveling toward. I can live loving and forgiving others. I can live telling others about His gift of sacrifice and salvation. I can live reflecting our Creator so others might see and believe.

Post script: Why did Christ's death have to be so horrible instead of just a quiet death? I'm beginning to wonder if it was not only a price to pay for our sin, but a great price for great sins. Sin is serious, and Christ's death was very serious. Our souls have great value, and He paid a high price for them. So should I or anyone not understand or believe the great value God puts on our souls, then look to the suffering of Christ.

The just shall live by his faith.

—Habakkuk 2:4 NKJV

# CHAPTER 11

## The Book of Habakkuk

### God's Simple but Profound Answer to Habakkuk's Distress

I read Habakkuk at a time when our country and the world were upside down. In our country alone, there was so much corruption in our governments, from local to federal. Our justice system had become corrupt as well…there was no justice anymore. We were experiencing food shortages, high gas prices as well as profound cultural shifts. When I first read Habakkuk, I was struck by the similarities of that culture and our own today.

> How long, O Lord, will I call for help and Thou wilt not hear? I cry out to Thee, "violence" yet Thou dost not save. Why dost Thou make me see iniquity and cause me to look on wickedness? Yes destruction and violence are before; Strife exists and contention arises.
> Therefore the law is ignored and justice is never upheld. For the wicked surround the righteous; Therefore, justice comes out perverted." (Habakkuk 1:1–4)

That is a picture of our world today. And we do cry out to God, but He seems silent. The wicked today are making alarming inroads into our culture and the hearts and minds of people.

Habakkuk asks God how He can look on evil for so long since He Himself is so pure. Then God speaks and says this:

> "Look among the nations and watch—be utterly astounded! For I will work a work in your days which you would not believe, though it were told you." (Habakkuk 1:5 NKJV)

He then goes on to say that a fierce people, the Chaldeans, are coming and will destroy and take captive the people. They will take homes and possessions.

This news is not good. But God soon gives this very simple but powerful answer to all of Habakkuk's questions and distress. God tells Habakkuk how to live through this coming judgment when He says, "The just shall live by his faith" (Habakkuk 2:4).

I'm not sure if Habakkuk was disappointed at first to hear this answer. He might have wanted a more detailed answer of how things were going to play out, what pain would people suffer, and when would it be over. But God was reminding Habakkuk that peace and comfort were to be found in his faith…a faith that seemed to stagger a bit. So I decided to look a little closer to the meaning of faith since it was God's only answer. Here's the biblical definition:

> Now faith is the assurance of things hoped for, the conviction of things not seen. (Hebrews 11:1 NASB)

So in the context of God's answer to Habakkuk to live by his faith, I think Habakkuk quickly saw what he needed to do. Habakkuk got caught up in the problems of the day as evil made terrible advances. But our loving God didn't condemn him for his lapse into his own human frailties but rather redirected his thoughts back to his faith. As a prophet of God, Habakkuk already had all the assurances and conviction he needed. But Habakkuk was also a human like all of us, and we forget as we get upset with things we desperately want changed but which instead get worse. Habakkuk needed God to remind him of his faith and direct him away from the problems. Sometimes, I need to be reminded, too, of who God is to recapture my assurances and convictions about Him. I find that if I go back and look again at God's character, I can more readily be comforted by assurances of things I hope for and conviction of things I have not seen.

1. God loves us and wants what's best for us.
2. God hears our prayers and answers them but in His way and His time.
3. God doesn't want us to fear things.
4. He is always victorious and carries us to that victory with Him.
5. God gives us hope, peace, joy, wisdom, discernment, armor to fight the enemy of our souls, His powerful Word, a path for our feet, a light for our way, strength for the journey, and His Holy Spirit to indwell and guide us.
6. God cannot lie, and His truth is powerful.

So when God told Habakkuk to live by his faith, it wasn't an unreasonable thing to ask. Habakkuk already knew God, so he could be assured that his hope in God was not in vain.

As to the conviction of things not seen, Habakkuk was very convinced that God existed or he never would have spoken to Him. He was himself appointed as a prophet of God. As for the rest of us, I think God has done works in each of our lives that bring us back to the belief in the reality of things hoped for and the evidence of things unseen. Habakkuk got back on track, and we all can as well.

I love the verse in Habakkuk 3:2 (NKJV), where he says to God this one thing: "In wrath remember mercy." I love it because we can always ask for mercy. In fact, in James 2:13 (NASB), it says, "Mercy triumphs over judgment."

In this short book, God brings Habakkuk back to a strong faith. It's a beautiful journey because it shows how much God cared about the spiritual well-being of Habakkuk over his physical well-being. And He cares about our spiritual well-being too. God knows that if our faith falters enough, it could be lost. In chapter 3:17–19, Habakkuk's faith speaks loud and clear as he comes to an understanding of God's appointed place of peace for him.

As Habakkuk accepts that God's judgment might include the loss of all things, he ends this book with the loving assurance that God will provide a way beyond our faith to navigate troubled times. It says that God will enable us to walk successfully through all the rough terrain that lies ahead. It's a beautiful picture of God's enabling grace.

> Though the fig tree does not bud
> and there are no grapes on the vines,
> though the olive crop fails
> and the fields produce no food,
> though there are no sheep in the pen
> and no cattle in the stalls,
> yet I will rejoice in the LORD,
> I will be joyful in God my Savior.
>
> The Sovereign LORD is my strength;
> he makes my feet like the feet of a deer,
> he enables me to tread on the heights. (Habakkuk 3:17–19 NIV)

Watch, stand fast in the faith, be brave, be strong.
Let all that you do be done with love.

—1 Corinthians 16:13 NKJV

# CHAPTER 12

## Watch, Stand Fast, Be Brave

### A Closer Look at 1 Corinthians 16:13

The more I get to know God, the more amazed I am at what seems to be His goal for our lives. That goal is to first trust Jesus for salvation, but then, moving forward, it's to show us how to live victoriously in a place where evil exists and where Satan prowls around, looking for someone to devour. The Corinthian passage is a snapshot of that.

1. Watch: Don't rush in with an uninformed opinion or bad attitude. Just watch, observe, analyze, and think.
2. Stand fast in the faith: Often, our faith is tested, or we begin to doubt or we forget about our faith altogether. By standing fast, we are guarding our faith so we won't lose it or let it diminish.
3. Be brave: It takes courage to be at odds with the rest of the people or to take a stand for something that's right when everyone else takes the easy way of just going along.
4. Be strong: Don't waiver. Know what you believe and why you believe it.
5. Let all you do be done in love: The best advice *ever*!

This is the real game changer, and here's why: In 1 Corinthians 13, we find an amazing definition of love. I'm going to paraphrase. If I don't have love, I just make a lot of noise. If I'm incredibly intelligent and I have the kind of faith that can move mountains, I am nothing without love. If I give away everything I have to help to feed and clothe the poor and give them shelter or if I go so far as to lay down my life for another but I don't have love, it profits me nothing.

So what then is love? Love is patient, love is kind, and is not jealous; love does not brag and is not arrogant, does not act unbecomingly; it does not seek its own, is not provoked, does not take into account a wrong suffered, does not rejoice in unrighteousness, but rejoices with the truth; it bears all things, believes all things, hopes all things, and endures all things. Love never fails (1 Corinthians 13:4–8 NASB).

If I learn anything from these verses, it's the important role love plays in everything. We are too weak on our own to live a life like what is described here. And we truly will never be perfect in this life, but we have a way marked out for us which will profoundly change us if we would but choose to follow what the scriptures are saying.

But no one says, "Where is God my Maker, Who gives songs in the night." (Job 35:10 NASB)

The Lord will command His loving kindness in the daytime and His song will be with me in the night. (Psalm 42:8 NASB)

I call to remembrance my song in the night; I meditate within my heart, and my spirit makes diligent search. (Psalm 77:6 NKJV)

# CHAPTER 13

## Songs in the Night

### God's Goodness in the Middle of a Sleepless Night

I had never heard before that God gave us His songs in the night. That fascinated me, and I wanted to explore what that meant. I think God's songs in the night are Him prompting us to forget our troubles for the moment and begin to focus on all that He has done for each of us. It becomes a quiet worship of Him as we remember His goodness. It's about finding peace, comfort, and, ultimately, rest from the worries of life, the hardships…all of it…because in the darkness, we can't literally see the sights that break our hearts and cause fear or hopelessness. Without those visuals, we can more easily turn our thoughts toward God and who He is and be comforted. I think I really like His night songs. The next time I can't sleep, I will praise His name and remember His goodness.

We who have fled for refuge in laying hold of the hope set before us. This hope we have as an anchor of the soul, a hope both sure and steadfast. (Hebrews 6:18–19 NKJV)

# CHAPTER 14

## The Anchor for Our Soul

### God's Gift of Hope in Troubled Times

 This is probably one of my favorite passages of Scripture. I believe the "hope" set before us is the work of Christ on the cross for our salvation. We have hope that we are in good hands, no matter what is happening around us. We have hope that we will be in heaven with God someday, and when life gets tough, even unbearable, this hope becomes an anchor for our soul. Our soul is securely bound to Christ and will not drift away when the storms of life come. If I was a tattooing kind of grandma, I might be tempted to have an anchor tattooed on my ankle…just for the opportunity to explain it to someone someday. On second thought, maybe a necklace is more my style.

The law of the Lord is perfect, restoring the soul; The testimony of the Lord is sure, making wise the simple. The precepts of the Lord are right, rejoicing the heart; The commandment of the Lord is pure, enlightening the eyes. (Psalm 19:7–8 NASB)

# CHAPTER 15

## Our Wonderful Counselor

### Our Wounded Souls Can Be Healed

These days, so many people are deeply wounded, confused, lost, and depressed. I love this passage of the Scripture because it points to our Great Counselor, a very present help in time of trouble. Look at all the help God offers each one of us for a multitude of afflictions or shortcomings. And what better counselor than the Lord Himself. In the book of Isaiah, God is telling us His many names. Here are just a few of them: Mighty God, Prince of Peace, and *Wonderful Counselor*.

Let's look at this Psalm. Here are God's areas of help that He offers:

1. His law restores our soul. Can you imagine if your soul is so wounded you don't think you'll ever be okay again and then God says this? His law distinguishes for us the things that are right and the things that are wrong.
2. His testimony makes us wise, no matter how ignorant we are. He tells us about Himself and shows us how to live in a fallen world.
3. His precepts (a general rule intended to regulate behavior or thought) make our hearts happy.
4. His commandments enlighten our eyes.

We can be assured that from God, we can be helped beyond anything a person can do for us or what we can do for ourselves. Our wounded souls can be healed. That is an amazing hope for all of us. We don't have to live in brokenness. We can gain new understanding, and with that new understanding, we can gain happiness and a godly perspective on everything. We can realize the very purpose for which we were born and know that it is God alone that places value on each one of us. God has provided a way for us to be a whole, happy, fulfilled person through His Word, His love, and His gifts of wisdom and understanding. And He says that if anyone lacks wisdom, let him ask of God, who gives generously and without reproach. Just ask.

Someday, all the wrongs will be righted, but in the meantime, God works His goodness in a broken world. We must understand the gravity of our sins against the holiness of God. So until Christ comes again, we will continue to see the brokenness and the battle that sin causes, but we will also see our merciful God working to bring goodness and healing in the thick of it all.

Thy Word is a Lamp unto my feet and a light for my path. (Psalm 119:105 KJV)

# CHAPTER 16

## A Lamp for My Feet

### You Can Know Where You're Going

This psalm speaks to the importance and power of God's word to us. This fallen world we live in can be a very dark place. How can we know how to make smart decisions? How can we feel confident about ourselves? What does real love look like? Why am I here in the first place? Where did I come from? Where am I going? Why did this or that bad thing happen to me? Why have I been betrayed by someone I know and love? There are so many questions that we will have over our lifetimes. Wouldn't it be wonderful to have one source that has all the answers? Actually, there is.

This psalm powerfully states, with full assurance, that His Word is a lamp unto our feet and a light for our path. Do you realize that the Bible (His Word) casts a light on where we presently are and a light on where we are heading? But there's more. The Bible also says this of itself: "All scripture is inspired by God and profitable for teaching, for reproof, for correction, and for training in righteousness, that the man of God may be complete, equipped for every good work" (2 Timothy 3:16–17).

We can know how to navigate this fallen world and find joy and peace, hope and assurance. We can know who we are, where we've come from, and where we are going.

For you formed my inward parts;
you knitted me together in my mother's womb.
I praise you, for I am fearfully and wonderfully made.
Wonderful are your works;
my soul knows it very well.
My frame was not hidden from you,
when I was being made in secret,
intricately woven in the depths of the earth.
Your eyes saw my unformed substance;
in your book were written, every one of them,
the days that were formed for me,
when as yet there was none of them. (Psalm 139:13–16 ESV)

# CHAPTER 17

## Psalm 139:13–16

### God is Passionately Preparing Every Life for Purpose

Never forget that all life is from God, and He is passionately preparing every life for purpose. He knows us intimately before we are even born. He is the one who forms us in the womb. We all matter to Him.

# CHAPTER 18

## My Prayer of Thanksgiving

### Thoughts on God's Eternal Word and How It Has Changed Me

Father, I just want to say thank you for Your written Word. Some have said it's a violent book. Some have tried to destroy it. Others have thought it was not relevant for today. Some say it's just too hard to understand. But I think it's beautiful. I think it's a book of unconditional love that brings Your story of redemption to life. It's where I have learned about how You created the heavens and the earth and all that is within them. Where You created us in Your own image and then breathed life into us. I think just that alone is amazing and awesome. In its pages, I see Your gentle ways and Your understanding of our weaknesses, yet You don't leave us weak but empower us to do Your will.

You've touched me personally with Your kindness and compassion, and that has helped me learn to love You more and more. I know if I don't understand something, I could ask You for wisdom, and You would give it abundantly and without reproach. You have taught me how to pray and about the value and power You give my prayers if my heart is seeking You. You have taught me about relationships and marriage, having a family, and teaching my children about You. You have blessed me over and over again. You have been my rescuer, and You have sent Your angel armies to fight Satan, the enemy of my soul. He is always prowling around, looking for someone to devour. You have promised that when the time would come to end this world and make all things new, that until then, You would help me fight this enemy. You have even given me instructions on how to fight and the armor to put on so I wouldn't be fatally wounded, and it has a shield of faith.

After all the years of my life, You have shown me Your unending love. I know that it's my faith in You that pleases You the most. I have learned in Your Word that it is always a good thing to believe in You and to trust You. Staying faithful pleases You. All the prophets in the Old Testament left so many examples of how Your chosen people were rebellious—sinful people who worshiped other gods, complained, were disobedient, and disrespectful. But You never abandoned them, and You never altered Your course with them. I used to wonder why You chose such a weak and rebellious people to call Your own, but then I realized that there are none to be found who are unlike Your chosen. And You never gave up on them, so I came to believe that You will never give up on anyone.

It is Your deep love for humanity that compels You to provide a way for any to be saved. No one is too bad or too lost that You aren't willing to redeem. I have learned all that about You from Your written Word. You said Your word will last through all eternity, and that's an awesome thing. Thank you. How beautiful You are.

Be anxious for nothing, but in everything by prayer and supplication, with thanksgiving, let your requests be made known to God and the peace of God which surpasses all understanding will guard your hearts and minds through Christ Jesus. (Philippians 4:6–7 NASB)

# CHAPTER 19

## Be Anxious for Nothing

### A Most Wonderful Blessedness Can Be Ours

For me, these words speak about a heavenly Father giving peace that passes all understanding as He tells us to be anxious for nothing. Peace that often comes at the most unexpected time and place but nevertheless comes. It brings joy, whose only source can be God himself because it is not silenced by the rocky uncertainties of this life. This joy cannot be lost to circumstances, events, and places. It can be felt in the darkest night as well as the brightest day. Peace and joy are not tangible or generated out of this life's various events. They just exist as a gift—unearned and attainable only through the grace of God to each of us. It can best be felt in those quiet places of our minds and hearts, and when felt, it brings healing and fearlessness. It will guard your heart and your mind through Christ Jesus. Joy and peace, when fully realized, cannot fail to bring to each of you the most wonderful blessedness. Our God cares for us. He is very good.

Therefore take up the whole armor of God, that you may be able to withstand in the evil day, and having done all, to stand.

Stand therefore, having girded your waist with truth, having put on the breastplate of righteousness, and having shod your feet with the preparation of the gospel of peace; above all, taking the shield of faith with which you will be able to quench all the fiery darts of the wicked one. And take the helmet of salvation, and the sword of the Spirit, which is the word of God. (Ephesians 6:13–17 NKJV)

# CHAPTER 20

## The Whole Armor of God

### Teaching Us How to Fight the Spiritual Battles on Earth

God knows the spiritual warfare that exists in this fallen world. But He has not left us without help or hope of winning against it. In His Word, He has laid out for us a plan to defeat the enemy of our souls—the devil. He tells us in 1 Peter 5:8 (NKJV) that "your adversary the devil walks about like a roaring lion, seeking whom he may devour." So it's real, and we need to pay attention.

Let's look closer at the imagery.

1. Gird your waist with truth. Truth must be kept close to you for it is what will distinguish for you what truth God speaks and what lies the devil speaks. Knowing and having the truth is vital. Truth itself is powerful.
2. The breastplate of righteousness. It covers your heart where your righteousness is found. Yours is a heart that Jesus has made right. Protect it in battle.
3. Shod your feed with the gospel of peace. Take the peace of God with you. It will keep you close to Him in the battle, and it will guard your heart and mind.

4. Shield of faith. Faith is powerful, so it is perfect to protect you from the fiery arrows of the devil that are meant to destroy you. Your faith reminds you who your Redeemer is.
5. Helmet of salvation. Your salvation is remembered in your mind. Protect your mind, lest you feel unworthy to be called God's child. The devil wants you to believe you are unworthy, so protect your mind in the battle.
6. The sword of the spirit, which is the Word of God. The Word is powerful and deadly toward evil, so it is represented as a sword. Jesus, when He was tempted in the wilderness by Satan, used scripture to respond to Satan's temptations; And Satan soon fled.

God has never left us defenseless. We can be fully protected as we live in this world. God bless you all.

I have heard of You by the hearing of the ear, but now my eye sees you. (Job 42:5 NKJV)

# CHAPTER 21

## The Book of Job

### (The Amazing Ending)

I've always found the book of Job to be puzzling. Why would God allow Satan to take everything from Job, including his children and his health, along with his fortunes, when He seemed to be very pleased with Job overall? As I've read and thought about this book a great deal, I began to understand that what looked like total destruction of Job's life was, instead, God's gift of revelation that would change his life forever in the best way possible.

The book begins with telling the reader that Job was the most righteous man in all the East. He was known for his integrity. His wealth was enormous, his family intact. When his seven sons and three daughters would gather together to eat and drink for days, Job covered any possible sin they might commit through sacrifice and prayer on their behalf. So what went wrong? With God's permission, Satan was allowed, piece by piece, to take all of Job's wealth, all his children, and, finally, Job's health. All this came out of the blue, unexpected, and, to Job's mind, undeserved. What Job didn't do in the story, however, was most important. He never cursed God.

His friends came by to sit with him in his utterly miserable state. No one spoke for days. When they did speak, it was not words of comfort as much as it was accusations that Job was suffering because he harbored hidden sin, and now God was punishing him. Job defended himself.

Then Job spoke, and his heart was puzzled about what he had done that God would do these terrible things. Job's life was in a very dark valley, and he needed comfort but instead got blame. He needed to talk to God and get his questions answered, but instead, there was silence. I can't imagine the painfulness of all of this. Physical pain was horrific, emotional pain was unbelievable, and spiritual pain was left unanswered. Somewhere in this story, Job did declare his belief, however, that he still knew that God was his redeemer. Music to God's ears, I think. But Job also wanted to die. Finally, God spoke, but I am puzzled all over again. He never mentioned anything to Job about this entire traumatic tragedy. Instead, God questioned Job but started by first telling Job to gird up his loins like a man. No sympathy there. God asked Job where he was when God laid the foundation of the earth. He asked Job if he was involved with anything that God created—the earth, the skies, the universe. Of course, Job couldn't answer and didn't even try.

Then God asked him what power did he have over creation. Could he do any of the things God could do?

Again, God used the words "gird up your loins like a man" as He asked Job if he could instruct God and annul His judgments. Did he have an arm like God and a voice that would thunder? He asked Job if he could protect and control the creatures that had been created with just a word. In other words, "Job, what could you do?" Answer: nothing like what God could do...absolutely nothing.

What followed was an awakening in Job as he truly saw God for the first time. This was the grand climax of this entire eventful book. Here is Job's beautiful and totally humble answer to all that God had asked him:

> "I know that You can do everything,
> And that no purpose of Yours can be withheld from You.
> You asked, 'Who is this who hides counsel without knowledge?'

> Therefore I have uttered what I did not understand,
> Things too wonderful for me, which I did not know.
> Listen, please, and let me speak.;
> You said, 'I will question you and you shall answer Me.'
>
> I have heard of You by the hearing of the ear,
> but now my eye sees You.
> Therefore I abhor myself,
> And repent in dust and ashes." (Job 42:1–6 NKJV)

If this had been my story, I might have been hardened against God by the time God had spoken. I might have been offended that no sympathy was offered, no comfort, no assurances. But Job reacted in total humility and understood for the first time that God was so much more than he ever believed or knew. He had only heard of God, but now, he had seen Him. A great respect for God flooded Job's heart. Job saw what he had failed to see before. His righteousness was through the law, but his repentance came because of the understanding that he was in the presence of an Almighty God. He gave honor to this magnificent God. I don't think Job was thinking about all he had been through at this time, but rather was overwhelmed with this new understanding of what a great God he was.

God then blessed Job with double the possessions he had lost plus seven more sons and three more daughters, and Job lived 140 years and saw four generations of his family. Job died an old man and full of days.

Job had a lot of questions throughout his suffering. I, too, find myself with a lot of questions about his suffering. It was wide sweeping and extremely intense and went on for some time. My first question is, What was the reason behind it all? I believe there are always layers of reasons, but the most obvious to me is this: Sometimes, there simply is no answer given because in our humanity, we lack the ability and knowledge to grasp a reason. And secondly, God is so complex and so big that I lack words to describe Him, let alone understand Him. We do understand, however, that even if we don't like it or think it's unfair, we all will suffer in this world because of the sin that is in the world. Sometimes, we'll suffer because of our own sinful choices, and sometimes, because the sin of others plays out against us in our own lives.

Whether we understand it or not, it will always be present in all of human life. It's an indisputable and unrelenting fact. So here's God's way to deal with it all. He wants us to understand that He won't be held accountable to us. His ways are certainly not our ways nor is the outcome what we would envision. His is always better. God allows suffering because it is where we often will seek for Him, where spiritual growth often occurs. We must understand that sin is the most destructive force in all the world. It separates us from God and will ultimately destroy us. We cannot think in terms of sin being equal to "just a little white lie," and we must understand that His nature is far above any accountability we might seek from Him.

As the story ends with blessings, I know it isn't enough to just hear about God. It's so important to see Him. When we see Him, I think our spirits will truly come alive. We can experience all that God wants to do in our lives that will bring us great joy and give Him great glory. We can have a close relationship that we would miss if we only heard about God and never really saw Him. I think it's amazing that God only addressed Job's real need and that was to understand how great his God really was. All the rest of Job's life before and after fell into its proper place because of this new revelation.

Let me leave you with this prophetic utterance from Job.

> "Oh, that my words were written! Oh that they were inscribed in a book! That with an iron stylus and lead they were engraved in the rock forever! And as for me, I know that my Redeemer lives and at the last He will take His stand on the earth." (Job 19:23–25 NKJV)

## NOT DONE YET

God fulfilled that desire in Job more than he could ever imagine. It has been recorded for all eternity! And here we are, reading about it and learning more about this wonderful God through Job's experiences. Amen, and amen.

# CHAPTER 22

## That Big Beautiful Moon

### My Special Song in the Night

> The people who walked in darkness
> Have seen a great light;
> Those who dwelt in the land of the shadow of death
> Upon them a light has shined.
>
> —Isaiah 9:2 NKJV

Life is tough, wouldn't you agree? The world can be a dark place with wars and displaced people, and here in this country, food and gas prices are soaring, supply chains are breaking down, housing is getting out of reach because of the rising costs, and then there are betrayals, abuses…the list is endless. And if I listen to too much news, it can be depressing or even overwhelming. I'm sure others have had times when they didn't know what they should do with their lives or if relationships can be fixed or if they can find a good-paying job… we can fill in the blank.

A while ago, I was feeling the heaviness of what's going on in the world. Then one evening, I stepped out onto my patio and I saw a huge beautiful full moon in the dark sky and I was so struck by its light. I never realized how bright the moon could be. I looked around me, and everything was more visible in the night. The ground was so much more visible... I could see my neighbor's yards better, and there were far fewer shadows. Everything was more visible, and I thought that this was exactly a picture of what the Bible meant when it said, "The people who were living in darkness have seen a great light." That "great light" was the coming of Christ to earth to bring hope to all. We're still living in a dark world, but the good news is God is still bringing His light into our life. The moon still shines in the dark sky to remind me again and again of God's presence, and I find comfort in that.

I've never felt my life has ever been in total darkness...the kind where there is absolutely no light or, to put it spiritually, no hope and no truth. But years ago, I got a glimpse of what that might look like. I was at a cabin, and it was a cloudy night, so there were no stars or moonlight. I woke up, and I couldn't see anything. I held my hand up in front of my face, and I literally could see nothing...no shadow of my hand...nothing. That was the absolute, most total darkness I've ever experienced, and I've never forgotten it.

These days, I find myself looking for the moon at night quite often now. I just love seeing it. I've noticed as the night progresses, the moon appears to be moving around my house. When I go to bed, I discovered it's right out my back door. If I wake up in the middle of the night, I see it by the side of my house. To me, this is just another metaphor of the all-encompassing presence of God.

One night, I couldn't sleep, so I got up and was walking around the house in the dark when I saw some unusual light on the floor of the bedroom. I looked out the window, and there was the moon, shining brightly into the bedroom. I just stood there, my mind full of thoughts of a faithful God who cared. I love the reminder it brings that all is not lost in this world...that we don't have to live in darkness if we know and belong to God. That there is hope...what a blessing that is...all these thoughts of hope and assurances are brought to mind by simply looking up and seeing the moon.

So here's a challenge for you. Google when the next full moon will occur, and if it's a clear night, step outside, look up, and be reminded that even though darkness is all around us, His light pierces that darkness.

Until next time... I hope you enjoy the moonlight.

# CHAPTER 23

## Consider This

### Short Snippets of Thoughtful Things

Some encouragement when you think the task is too much, the mountain too high, the valley too deep...from a little snail and a quote by Charles Spurgeon, a famous theologian:

By perseverance, the snail reached the ark.

One generation will declare Your works to the next and will proclaim Your mighty acts. (Psalm 145:4 CSB)

I believe that God's name and the things He does will be declared until the end of time. And until then, we also have this promise:

His truth endures to all generations. (Psalm 100:5 NKJV)

We will never have a time when His truth cannot be known. He so well equips us for life in this world so we can live for Him, declare

Him to the next generation, and be guided by His truth forever. I love that.

## There Is Something Grand in the Littles

When I find myself in troubled times and pray for an end to such times, I often forget to notice the "littles" of God...those moments of small blessings along the way through the valley. I wish I didn't miss these blessings so much. God often takes a long time to answer prayers about big issues or troubles, and waiting is often the hardest thing to do. But God often gives many little blessings and comforts along the way. I want to be able to see those things and give Him my thanks and let those blessings have their moment in my life to encourage and refresh me. I try to notice the "littles," and when I do, I find my faith is not so tested.

> Keep your heart with all diligence for out of it spring the issues of life. (Proverbs 4:23 NKJV)

> He has shown you, O man, what is good;
> And what does the Lord require of you
> But to *do justly*,
> To *love mercy*,
> And to *walk humbly with your God*? (Micah 6:8 NKJV)

> Do not withhold good from those to whom it is due, when it is in the power of your hand to do so. (Proverbs 3:27 NKJV)

> These six things the Lord hates,
> Yes, seven are an abomination to Him:
> A proud look,
> A lying tongue,
> Hands that shed innocent blood,
> A heart that devises wicked plans,

Feet that are swift in running to evil,
A false witness who speaks lies,
And one who sows discord among the brethren. (Proverbs 6:16–19 NKJV)

For we have brought nothing into the world, so we cannot take anything out of it either. (1 Timothy 6:7 NASB)

A good name is to be more desired that great riches, favor is better than silver and gold. (Proverbs 22:1 NASB)

O give us help against our adversary, For deliverance by man is in vain. Through God we shall do valiantly and it is He who will tread down our adversaries. (Psalm 60:11–12 NASB)

I love the phrase, "through God, we will do valiantly." That is so comforting to me. That's not just doing well…it's doing well courageously and with determination. We will thrive in this troubled world if we have God as our Father. He makes us able to live our lives valiantly. Awesome!

Thanksgiving…time to remember how blessed we are and to be really thankful. So when asked what you're thankful for, phrase the answer like this: "I'm thankful for 'fill in the blank' *because*." Adding because changes things a bit, don't you agree? It's easy to say I'm thankful for my family, but when we add *because*, it goes deeper. And hearing the "because" can change everything.

Where would we all be if Jesus hadn't been born? It is God's Spirit who holds back the evil one from completely annihilating us. The evil in the world today is great, but if it has no pushback, I can't even imagine what life would be like. We so desperately need a Savior, and I am so very thankful we have one. It's terribly sad that so many refuse to even consider Jesus or, worse yet, after considering Him, totally reject Him. The story of Jesus's birth is so amazing. He's the Creator, and yet, He became the sacrifice as well. No one can love another like that. My prayer is for all to reside under the protection and love of God Himself…in the shelter of His wings.

Let us eat and be merry for this my son was dead and is alive again; he was lost and is found.

—Luke 15:23–24 NKJV

# CHAPTER 24

## The Story of the Prodigal Son

### You Can Always Come Home

I want to end this little book with this story as a way to encourage you and to let you know you can never be too lost to redeem and God always wants to redeem us. It's the story of The Prodigal Son. It's found in Luke 15:11–24.

> Jesus continued: "There was a man who had two sons. The younger one said to his father, 'Father, give me my share of the estate.' So he divided his property between them.
>
> "Not long after that, the younger son got together all he had, set off for a distant country and there squandered his wealth in wild living. After he had spent everything, there was a severe famine in that whole country, and he began to be in need. So he went and hired himself out to a citizen of that country, who sent him to his fields to feed pigs. He longed to fill his stomach with the pods that the pigs were eating, but no one gave him anything.
>
> "When he came to his senses, he said, 'How many of my father's hired servants have food to

spare, and here I am starving to death! I will set out and go back to my father and say to him: Father, I have sinned against heaven and against you. I am no longer worthy to be called your son; make me like one of your hired servants.' So he got up and went to his father.

"But while he was still a long way off, his father saw him and was filled with compassion for him; he ran to his son, threw his arms around him and kissed him.

"The son said to him, 'Father, I have sinned against heaven and against you. I am no longer worthy to be called your son.'

"But the father said to his servants, 'Quick! Bring the best robe and put it on him. Put a ring on his finger and sandals on his feet. Bring the fattened calf and kill it. Let's have a feast and celebrate. For this son of mine was dead and is alive again; he was lost and is found.' So they began to celebrate."

There's a bit more to the story, but for the sake of space and time, I want to comment on just this part.

We all stray from God at times. We want to be our own person, to do what we want, to have fun, and to escape the drama/trauma of life, but God knows that will ultimately lead us farther from Him and closer to Satan. God knows of the hardships of life, the losses we'll encounter, and the sadness and hopelessness. But He's more than willing and able to walk through these times with us so we can be overcomers. Satan is also willing to walk through these times with us, only his plan is to use these moments to destroy us. Satan begins by telling us it'll be fun. God begins by warning us of the dangers. Satan twists bad things to look good while God lays straight the right path right in front of us.

Two very important things in this story I don't want to miss. The first is that the son understood his sins and repented before he returned home. And the second was that the Father was ready to forgive and restore his son, so much so that when he saw him, he ran to embrace him. He didn't condemn him; rather, he exclaimed with great joy: "This son of mine was dead and has come to life again. He was lost and has been found." Those beautiful words will still be said over any of us who have strayed away from God and come back. This is the most hopeful story, full of God's grace and unconditional love, and you will find that God has kept your place at His table. If you are far away from God, come home. All of heaven is waiting to rejoice.

# EPILOGUE

This little book has reached its end, but my story has not. It will go on into eternity as will all our stories. I want to keep learning from God and interacting with Him. What a privilege that is. In the Bible, He calls Himself "I Am" because He is everything to all things. There is none like Him. None to compare Him to. I hope that the things I've written about are the things you've wondered about. It has been my intention from the beginning to leave the truths and understanding that I've come to know with all of you and the prayer that it will become a "pass-along book" to the next generation. All of you, my dear family, have meant the world to me. I'm so proud of you. God bless you.

# ABOUT THE AUTHOR

In her wildest dreams, Carol never thought she would write a book and have it published. She feels this is one of those "God surprises" that is intimidating yet irresistibly exciting. Many years ago, when trying to decide on a career, she soon realized that staying home and being a full-time wife and mother fit her well. In those years, she volunteered at innumerable things, but her greatest achievement, ultimately, was sharing her faith with her family and then seeing them each make the decision to follow Jesus as their Lord and Savior.

Having a full day of time to choose what she did was wonderful but also required a large measure of self-discipline, if those years were to be well spent. However, she will be the first to admit it was challenging at times. Being consistently a part of a women's Bible Study offered many opportunities to learn and grow as a Christian. She credits her growing faith with this powerful connection to God. She will tell you that these years gave her many opportunities to pray more consistently, which has made a positive difference in her life.

She enjoys her hobbies of sewing, quilting, and knitting. She has been married to her husband, Bob for fifty-five years, and together, they share three children, nine grandchildren and four great-grandchildren. God is good. They are Michiganders who transplanted to Nashville, Tennessee, eight years ago.

Printed in the USA
CPSIA information can be obtained
at www.ICGtesting.com
LVHW021253190424
777772LV00002B/447